The Steel Donkey

A Tale from Barbados

K.N. Chimbiri

Illustrated by Sanjay Charlton

Hachette UK's policy is to use papers that are natural, renewable and recyclable products and made from wood grown in well-managed forests and other controlled sources. The logging and manufacturing processes are expected to conform to the environmental regulations of the country of origin.

ISBN: 9781398377349

Text © K.N. Chimbiri
Illustrations, design and layout © Hodder & Stoughton Limited
First published in 2023 by Hodder Education Group,
An Hachette UK Company
Carmelite House, 50 Victoria Embankment, London EC4Y 0DZ
www.risingstars-uk.com

Impression number 10 9 8 7 6 5 4 3 2 1
Year 2027 2026 2025 2024 2023

Author: K.N. Chimbiri
Series Editor: Catherine Coe
Commissioning Editor: Hamish Baxter
Cover Illustrator: Tika and Tata/Bright Group International
Internal Illustrator: Sanjay Charlton/Beehive
Educational Reviewer: Pauline Allen
Design: Gary Kilpatrick
Page layouts: Lorraine Inglis
Editor: Amy Tyrer

With thanks to the schools that took part in the development of *Reading Planet Cosmos*, including: Ancaster CE Primary School, Ancaster; Downsway Primary School, Reading; Ferry Lane Primary School, London; Foxborough Primary School, Slough; Griffin Park Primary School, Blackburn; St Barnabas CE First & Middle School, Pershore; Tranmoor Primary School, Doncaster; and Wilton CE Primary School, Wilton.

A catalogue record for this title is available from the British Library.

Printed in India.

All rights reserved. Apart from any use permitted under UK copyright law, no part of this publication may be reproduced or transmitted in any form or by any means, electronic or mechanical, including photocopying and recording, or held within any information storage and retrieval system, without permission in writing from the publisher or under licence from the Copyright Licensing Agency Limited. Further details of such licences (for reprographic reproduction) may be obtained from the Copyright Licensing Agency Limited, www.cla.co.uk/

Orders: Please contact Hachette UK Distribution, Hely Hutchinson Centre, Milton Road, Didcot, Oxfordshire, OX11 7HH.
Telephone: (44) 01235 400555. Email: primary@hachette.co.uk.

Contents

Chapter 1 4

Chapter 2 11

Chapter 3 21

Chapter 4 31

Chapter 5 34

Chapter 6 42

Chapter 1

"I can do it myself, Mum," I said.

Yes, I was only ten years old, but I could cornrow my hair myself. I could even manage the back.

"No, Akeenah. You're taking too long," Mum said. She whisked the wide-toothed comb out of my hand. "Let me finish it for you."

Mum was a hairdresser at Rita's Beauty Salon near town, one of the best salons on the island. She loved her job.

Mum plaited seven perfectly straight cornrows into the back of my hair. They matched my front rows exactly. She tied an orange ribbon to the top of my hair with a flourish. "Looks great, even if I do say so myself."

"Thanks, Mum."

I went to my bedroom to change into my school uniform – a short-sleeved white blouse and an orange pinafore dress with purple trimming. Shafts of golden sunlight streamed through the net curtain, casting shadows onto the dark wood of my wardrobe. I turned on the fan as I dressed.

Then, I went into the kitchen and took a small carton of guava juice out of the freezer. *Nice!* I thought. It was frozen solid. I grabbed my lunch box from the counter and put everything into my haversack. I paused on the mat by the door to slip on my white socks and black school shoes, before heading out.

"See you later, Mum."

It was just after eight in the morning, but it was warm already. I walked very slowly. I hated getting too sweaty before I got to school.

As I got to the main road, I saw my cousin Derrell jogging to our meeting point. *He's going to be complaining soon that it's too hot,* I thought.

5

Derrell's mum, Auntie Adele, and my mum were sisters. They had an older brother, Uncle Joseph. He didn't talk much. The three of them grew up in Elverton, but only Uncle Joseph had moved away. Like our mums, Derrell and I had always lived in Elverton.

Although the road wasn't busy, Derrell looked both ways and crossed carefully, as usual.

"Yeah, cuz," he said cheerily, as he came towards me.

"Yeah, cuz," I greeted him in return, and we began to walk towards our schools.

I went to Elverton Girls' Primary School. Derrell went to the boys' school next door.

After we'd walked for less than five minutes, Derrell exclaimed, "Look! I'm dripping with sweat." He lifted up one of his arms to reveal a sweat patch on his orange shirt.

"Yuk, Derrell, that's so disgusting."

He laughed.

We approached Mr and Mrs Forde's house. Mrs Forde was in the large front garden. As usual, Mr Forde was nowhere to be seen. The Fordes had one of the most colourful gardens in Elverton. It was bursting with leafy crotons, hibiscus and bougainvillea in many colours.

"Mornin' Mrs Forde," we said in unison as we walked past.

She wiped her brow with the back of her hand and squinted at us. "Mornin' children."

She always called us 'children' even though she knew our names. Like many people in Elverton, Mrs Forde was a distant relative of ours in some way.

A hummingbird hovered gracefully above a cluster of fuchsia flowers. I wanted to admire the garden, but I turned my attention to the wrought iron man's shop on the other side of the road. The place always creeped me out because it was the only place in Elverton that always looked deserted.

The wrought iron shop was made of four long, thin planks of knotted pine, staked upright in the ground. Rough wooden beams were balanced on top of the planks to form a ceiling which looked like a 3-D noughts and crosses grid. The roof was just a sheet of tarpaulin tossed over the ceiling beams.

Huge hooks hung down from the ceiling beams. A few of the hooks held painted white window grilles. An old wooden workbench stood at the centre of the shop. A faded, battered sign was propped up against one of its legs. It read: 'Ormonde's Wrought Iron and Metal Works'.

The little wooden house next to the shop looked like it might just collapse at any moment. Any paint decoration it once enjoyed had faded away years ago. As always, the windows were shuttered tight. A couple of light-grey cement blocks were lying by the side of the house. Next to them were several tattered cardboard boxes of screws, lying open on their sides.

Beyond the house and shop I saw the tall, wild grass of an overgrown pasture.

"How could anyone possibly live here when it's always shut up?" I'd said once.

"Because they're trying to keep people out and they're hiding a big secret," Derrell had replied in a spooky voice. He'd tried to scare me but he just sounded so ridiculous. I'd burst out laughing, but I couldn't help feeling uneasy. *Why was the house always closed up?* I wondered.

Since that day, Derrell began spinning more and more scary tales about the inhabitants of the broken-down house next to the wrought iron shop.

I heard a low creaking noise. What was that sound? Despite the heat, I shivered with fear. Derrell laughed. "You're such a scaredy cat."

My body stiffened as I heard the sound again. This time, I saw the freshly painted window grilles moving. They made the creaking sound as the wind swung them back and forth. I really was too jumpy.

"Oh, that cool breeze feels good," Derrell said, holding his shirt collar away from his body as if to capture all the wind.

We passed Col's Mini Mart, turned on to Rawlins Road and my school came into view.

"What are you doing at the weekend, cuz?" Derrell asked.

"On Sunday afternoon we're going on an excursion," I said.

Derrell looked impressed.

"There's going to be 30 people – the other hairstylists from the salon and their families. My mum is making the rice and peas."

"Will your dad be back in time?"

"As long as his flight isn't late." My dad worked for Cool Breeze Airconditioning. He was away in Puerto Rico on business until Sunday morning, visiting their most important client.

"Later, cuz!" Derrell said, as he dashed off to his school. I headed into mine.

I really was looking forward to the weekend. Little did I know that it would turn out to be the scariest time of my whole life.

Chapter 2

That night, Mum and I spoke to Dad on the phone, had our showers and headed to bed. As I pulled the curtains in my room closed, I saw a chalky-white moon high in the night sky.

I was in a deep sleep when something woke me up.

What's that? Thunder? I thought, although I'd never heard such loud thunder before in all my life.

Walking over to the window, I pulled back one of the curtains to peek outside. The window pane was bone-dry. No rain. All I could hear was the usual chirping crickets and whistling frogs.

Reassured, I headed back to bed.

THUD. THUD. THUD.

My heart began to hammer in my chest and all my senses were alert. Seconds later, the window panes began to rattle, and fear flooded through me. Then, my whole bedroom began to shake.

Mum burst through the door, her eyes wide with terror.

"It's the Steel Donkey!" she screamed, pulling me roughly out of the room. Stunned and confused, I barely had time to grab my slippers before we raced out of the house.

Out of the corner of my eye, I thought I glimpsed something in the shadows. Something metallic. But Mum urged us on, holding my hand so hard that it really hurt.

"Run, Akeenah, run!"

I ran as fast as I could with my slippers on.

Behind us came a strange scraping sound. I felt a blast of hot air on my back. My nightdress felt heavy and sticky against my skin. My feet were sweaty and slippery.

Mum shouted, "Run faster!" Her voice sounded hoarse.

My slippers made squelching sounds as they pounded the ground. I was so out of breath I could barely speak. "Mum … What's … Going … On?"

"Keep running." There was no time to stop. The sounds were getting louder and louder.

"Quick! Hide over there." Mum shoved me so hard I almost fell. Then she was gone.

My surroundings seemed familiar. Then I realised that I was in the wrought iron man's shop.

I can't stay here, I thought. I wanted to run out of the shop, but I heard the scraping noise getting louder and louder.

I looked around frantically for a hiding place. I dashed towards the workbench in front of me and crouched down behind one of its narrow back legs. I tried to make myself as small as possible, but it was no use. I needed to find a place that would conceal me properly. As I stood up, I saw something moving – like a dark shadow against the night. I gasped as I realised that two fiery-red eyes were glowing menacingly at me in the dim moonlight.

I backed away slowly from the workbench. My heart was pounding in my chest and I could feel the blood pulsing in my temples. I knew I had to run for my life. I spun around and tried to escape.

"Oww!" I screamed.

I tripped over something. I saw screws go flying and spill out over the ground in front of me. As I fell over, I put out my hands to try to break my fall. The palm of one of my hands slammed into a screw.

"Oww!" I screamed again, now face down on the ground. The pain was intense. I rolled over on my back and half sat up. I looked around, straining my eyes in the dark as I tried to see where the shadowy creature was. I saw its eyes getting closer and closer. I used my sore hands and trembling legs to push myself backwards along the ground, trying to create as much distance as possible between the creature and me.

In the moonlight, I could see the eyes were set into an animal's face.

This must be the Steel Donkey, I thought. The hairs on my arms stood up as the beast moved steadily closer to me. I seized my chance before it was too late. I scrambled to my feet, spun around and sprinted as fast as my weak legs would let me.

I ran behind the deserted house next to the shop and pressed myself against the wall. My heart was still beating rapidly. I took deep breaths as I tried to calm myself down. Where was the Steel Donkey now? I risked poking my head out from the back of the house to take a peek.

I saw the Steel Donkey's eyes and then a quick flash of fire. I thought I saw it staring at the screws I'd scattered as I fell. A wheezy voice said, "Forty-five. Forty-six. Forty-seven …"

Suddenly I heard a dull click, like someone snapping their fingers.

What was that? I thought. A light came shining through a crack in one of the shutters above my head. I realised that someone was in the empty house!

I didn't wait to find out any more. I knew I had to get away. I ran wildly through the tall grass. The moonlight cast a chalky-white glow over the ground in front of me. My slippers clapped noisily against my sweaty heels.

I thought I heard something behind me, but it was just a strong gust of wind rustling the tree leaves. A wave of relief washed over my body.

I slowed my pace and glanced backwards. When I turned around … SLAM. I ran straight into a tall figure.

"Mum!"

"Akeenah! My baby. Are you okay?" She crouched down and hugged me so tightly that I could scarcely breathe. "Are you okay?"

I hugged her back just as tightly. "Yes," I answered breathlessly. I could only manage a one-word reply.

"I'm so sorry," Mum cried. "I tried to lead it away from you but it stopped following me. I came back past the wrought iron shop but I couldn't see you. I thought you might try to get to your Auntie Adele's."

I looked over Mum's shoulder and saw Derrell's house. I hadn't been thinking about where I was going, but as if on autopilot I'd run towards Derrell's.

I caught my breath and managed a few words. "Is it following me?"

"I don't see it," Mum replied. "Let's get inside."

We scampered up the front steps and Mum tapped on the front door. She looked back towards the pasture, her eyes scanning the darkness. She tapped on the door again repeatedly until, after a few minutes, Auntie Adele's face appeared at the side window. Then, she disappeared and it felt like ages before she opened the door.

"Alison? What's wrong?" Auntie Adele asked Mum.

"The Steel Donkey," Mum replied in a hushed voice.

Auntie Adele's sleepy eyes widened. Mum pushed past her and sank down heavily into the green sofa in the living room. I slumped down next to her and she clasped my hand. Auntie Adele pulled out a chair from the table and sat down opposite us.

"Are you okay, Alison?" Auntie Adele asked. She got up almost as soon as she'd sat down. "Do you want some water?" Without waiting for our replies, she disappeared into the kitchen. Uncle Raymond came out of the bedroom rubbing his eyes.

"What's going on? Alison? Akeenah?"

Auntie Adele walked back into the room with two large glasses. She looked at Uncle Raymond.

"The Steel Donkey," she told him.

Mum gripped my hand even tighter. We took the glasses from Auntie Adele with our free hands.

My hands were shaking so badly that I spilled most of my water. I managed to take a few sips and found my voice again.

"What's the Steel Donkey? Why is it chasing us?" I asked.

Mum suddenly released my hand from her vice-like grip.

"Time for bed, Akeenah. You've been through enough. There's nothing for you to worry about. We'll take care of it."

"Yes. Yes," Auntie Adele chimed in. "You and your mum will sleep with me. Raymond, you sleep out here. No need to wake up Derrell."

Uncle Raymond disappeared into the main bedroom and came back with a pillow in his arms. Mum and I got up off the sofa.

I asked again about the Steel Donkey but the response was still the same – silence.

"Enough, Akeenah." Mum gently but firmly pushed me into the bedroom.

"Sleep in the middle of the bed. Auntie Adele and I will come in later." She walked over to the window and looked out for a while before she left the room.

"Good night, Akeenah," she sighed.

As I lay in bed I could hear the three of them talking in low hushed tones. I strained to hear but I couldn't make out any of their words. I thought about getting out of bed and listening at the door, but I felt too exhausted.

Soon I drifted off into a fitful sleep.

Chapter 3

"Akeenah. Wake up." Mum was shaking my shoulders vigorously.

"Let's go," she whispered. "Try not to wake up your auntie. She's hardly had any sleep."

Warm, bright sunlight streamed into the room. Auntie Adele was on her side on the edge of the bed, snoring loudly. We tiptoed quietly out of the room, past the closed door of Derrell's room and into the living room. Uncle Raymond was fast asleep on his front on the sofa. One leg was bent so that his foot was rested on the sofa arm, while the other leg dangled off the sofa on to the floor. A floorboard squeaked as we inched gingerly towards the front door. Uncle Raymond shifted slightly, but he didn't wake up.

I blinked in the bright sunlight when we stepped out onto the top step. Mum pushed the front door slowly and carefully, so it barely made a noise when it closed.

As we headed home, Mum broke the bad news to me: "Akeenah, we're going away to stay with Uncle Joseph."

"What? Why? When?"

"This evening."

"For how long?"

"For a while, Akeenah. For a while."

I didn't like the direction of this conversation. "But I don't want to go to Uncle Joseph's." My voice was high-pitched. "Is this because of the Steel Donkey?"

"Akeenah, the Steel Donkey came to our house last night. It's a menace to the home it targets, and it likes to come out at night. We need to be somewhere else for a while."

"Can't we stay with Auntie Adele and Uncle Raymond?" I was sure they wouldn't mind.

"They haven't got the room. Uncle Joseph has space."

There were many good reasons not to go to Uncle Joseph's. For one, Uncle Joseph lived on the other side of the island. He'd moved out of Elverton a few years ago to buy a chicken farm. We visited last year for the weekend, and those chickens were up so early there was no chance of a lie-in. Mum loved to have her lie-ins. Then there was school. It would be too far to walk to school from Uncle Joseph's. I began to point out these obvious problems, but Mum wouldn't listen to reason.

"Akeenah! I. Am. Tired," she said each word pointedly. "I can't discuss this right now. Just trust me."

We walked the rest of the way in silence. Thoughts swirled around in my mind as I continued to ponder our situation.

We turned onto our road. I tensed as the memories of last night came flooding back. We approached our house and I felt relieved to see that it looked normal.

"Don't worry," Mum said as if she'd read my thoughts. "The Steel Donkey won't be here. It's daytime."

Still, I felt nervous as I followed Mum inside. She picked up a wedding photo which must have been knocked to the floor when the Steel Donkey came last night.

"There," she said to herself, as she put it back on the shelf. She rearranged a few books on the shelf above that were lying on their side, and then disappeared into the kitchen.

I showered, put on my body lotion and pulled on an old white T-shirt and a green skirt. I began to replay last night's events in my mind as I came back into the living room.

Two plates of pasta salad were already on the table. After we devoured our food, Mum said, "It won't be so bad at Uncle Joseph's, you'll see."

"How do you know the Steel Donkey won't follow us there?"

"Akeenah. I don't want you to worry," Mum said.

We spent half the night being chased by a creature and my life's been turned upside down. There's just a little bit to worry about, I thought.

"I'm not a little baby, you know. I'm ten years old," I pointed out.

Mum smiled.

Before I could ask more questions, I heard a voice outside.

"Afternoon."

"Cuz?" I ran to the door and flung it open.

"Afternoon, Derrell," Mum said. She got up and looked at her phone. "Look at the time! I still have to call a taxi, pack for us, and top-up my phone. Oh! I've so much to do!"

Mum got her purse and fished out a twenty-dollar bill.

"Derrell, Akeenah, go to Col's and get a twenty-dollar top-up for me please." Mum pushed the money into my hand.

"Cuz, what's going on?" Derrell asked as soon as we were on our way to Col's Mini Mart.

"Didn't you hear anything last night?"

"No. I was fast asleep. This morning I saw my dad on the couch and Mum told me you came over last night," Derrell said. "I asked her why but she just said she'd explain later and asked me to come over here."

As I began to recount last night's events, Derrell's eyes widened with disbelief. I told him how we were chased by the creature, how I ended up in the shop hiding, and then how I'd fled to his house.

"What did it look like?" he asked.

"I couldn't see it properly in the dark, but it made a strange clanging noise. I only saw its eyes. They were horrible." I shivered as I remembered the eyes glowing like embers in the dark.

Derrell's mouth fell so wide open I thought it would fall off its hinges.

"And you ended up here?" Derrell asked, turning his head towards the wrought iron shop.

I was so busy talking to Derrell that I hadn't realised we'd already passed Mr and Mrs Forde's house. A knot formed in the pit of my stomach as I followed his gaze across the road.

As I looked over, Derrell's words echoed my thoughts: *"But it looks the same as when we walked home from school yesterday."*

He was right! Nothing looked out of place. Some of the grilles were gone, but the wrought iron man's shop looked as messy as usual. It certainly didn't look any worse.

The house next to the shop looked exactly the same as it always did.

"There was definitely something or someone in the house last night," I told Derrell.

"Really?"

"Yes. When I was hiding behind the house I saw a light come on," I continued. "You know, I just can't help wondering now if there's a connection between the Steel Donkey and this shop."

Derrell didn't reply, but we sped up our walking pace and reached Col's Mini Mart in record time.

Cars were parked on both sides of the road outside the shop. Col's was always busy, especially on Saturday afternoons. Since it could only hold six cars, the small paved car park in front of the mini mart was already full. We joined the people waiting to buy top-ups at the brightly painted orange wooden kiosk outside the shop. I didn't recognise anyone. They were probably people from outside Elverton who'd just stopped on their way to town or the airport.

Soon it was our turn to be served and I asked for the phone top-up.

The cashier handed us her notebook and pen and grunted, "Write down the number."

I scrawled down my mum's phone number and handed it up to her along with the $20 bill. She put our top-up into her machine and wordlessly held out the receipt for me.

As we left Col's, Derrell said, "Let's walk back and take a closer look at the wrought iron man's shop."

"Are you serious, cuz?" My mouth suddenly felt dry and I could feel panic rising through my body.

"Your mum said the Steel Donkey only comes out at night," Derrell reasoned. "Maybe we can find out more about this Steel Donkey business."

I couldn't think of a reply, but I felt more and more uneasy with every step.

We reached the wrought iron shop. A little Sparky perched on the top of a door grille watching us. It darted away.

I pointed to the workbench. "That's where I was hiding." In the daylight I could see that the ground around the workbench area was cracked and dry. We moved in closer and I saw torn oily rags and some kind of tool on the workbench.

"That angle grinder looks expensive," Derrell said.

"How do you know that?" I asked Derrell.

"My dad has one," he replied. Derrell's dad, Uncle Raymond, was a builder. "He uses it to cut the steel rods."

Steel rods? I thought. *There just must be some connection with the Steel Donkey.*

I nervously followed Derrell as he moved to look around behind the workbench. I saw an overturned stool and thought to myself: *That must be what I fell over last night.* Screws were strewn around.

"Look, cuz. The screws are still here," I said. I told Derrell how I'd tripped, spilling the screws. "The Steel Donkey was really interested in them."

"And that's when it stopped following you?" he asked.

"I guess so," I replied. "I know it sounds strange, but I thought I heard counting."

"Huh?" Derrell said.

I felt sick as I recalled the whole experience.

"I think we should go now, cuz," I said.

But Derrell wasn't listening. He was dashing towards the front of the broken-down house, next to the shop.

"Wait!" I shouted at him.

"I'm taking a closer look," Derrell said. "Don't be scared. We need to get to the bottom of this mystery."

I swallowed my fear and slowly followed Derrell.

I couldn't believe he was walking up to the house. I was watching him so intently that I didn't hear someone creeping up on us. I jumped when I heard a voice behind me.

Chapter 4

"What are you children doing here?" It was just Mrs Forde from across the road. "Are you looking for Ormonde, who owns the shop? He's not in."

"We're looking for the Steel Donkey," Derrell blurted out.

Mrs Forde looked at us. "What do you children know about the Steel Donkey?"

"It was here last night," I said. "I saw it."

"I told Mr Forde that I heard something over here," Mrs Forde said. "But when I looked out, I didn't see anything. Tell me what happened."

I told Mrs Forde everything. She listened intently, nodding her head.

"The Steel Donkey hasn't got anything to do with Ormonde or his shop," she said when I had finished my tale.

"I never thought it did," said Derrell.

Oh, yes you did, I thought.

"We never see Ormonde at the shop and the house is always closed up," I pointed out. "Why?"

"The Steel Donkey just came here because you were here and it followed you," Mrs Forde explained. "You never see Ormonde because he leaves early in the morning to drive to his customers. He goes all over the island you know, and works very long hours."

"Why was the Steel Donkey chasing me, Mrs Forde?" I asked.

"No one really knows," she said. "It just appears randomly and it's a menace to those it targets."

"But that's not fair," I cried. "Is there nothing we can do?"

Mrs Forde shook her head from side to side.

Derrell and I said goodbye to Mrs Forde and headed home.

Looks like I'll be leaving Elverton then, I thought to myself, sadly.

"Maybe it won't be for long," Derrell said, as though he'd read my thoughts, but he didn't really sound convinced.

We walked the rest of the way in silence. The hot Barbados sun beat down on us.

I glanced over at Derrell a few times. He looked dejected and kept his head down as he walked. A couple of times he kicked a stone with his shoe.

I thought he was going to say something, but whenever I glanced over, he was just muttering to himself or shaking his head. Once he let out such a deep sigh it made his shoulders go up and down.

We reached the corner where we'd go our own ways. We looked at each other.

"Later, cuz," Derrell said.

"Yeah, later," I replied. I watched him walking towards his house and I sighed too. Derrell could be a pain sometimes, but I would really miss him. I felt useless, weak and powerless.

Chapter 5

Later that afternoon, I was sitting outside on the front step. I saw Derrell, Auntie Adele and Uncle Raymond walking towards me.

"Afternoon, Akeenah," Auntie Adele said. I stood up and she gave me a big hug. She and Uncle Raymond went inside and I sat back down on the step. Derrell flopped down next to me. I felt really pleased that he was here.

After a while I heard Uncle Raymond ask: "Where is this taxi?"

"Call him, Alison," I heard Auntie Adele say to Mum.

"I'm trying." Mum sounded stressed. "There's no answer."

Mum recounted how she couldn't find anyone to give her a lift and had to arrange a taxi instead.

"Cruise ships and lots of tourists arrive on Saturdays, you know," I heard her say. "I had so much trouble finding a taxi on a Saturday at such short notice."

Finally, the taxi pulled up. The driver got out and walked around to the trunk of his white car, which was encrusted with dirt. Someone had traced some words with their fingertip on the side: 'CLEAN ME'.

"Evenin'," the driver said cheerily, as he came towards us.

"You're late," Mum said, as she came out of the house.

"Sorry, ma'am. I had an airport pick-up but the flight was delayed," the driver replied.

Derrell and I got out of the way as Uncle Raymond, Auntie Adele and Mum came down the stairs. I watched as Uncle Raymond brought out a suitcase in each hand and helped the driver put them in the trunk.

Auntie Adele followed him, giving suggestions on how to arrange the two cases. I saw Mum lock the front door and drop the keys into her handbag. She opened the car's back door and threw her bag on the seat. Then, she came over and hugged Derrell.

"Come on, Akeenah. Hurry up and get in," she told me. "Adele, Raymond, I will ring you later when we get to Joe's."

The driver slammed the trunk shut and got in his seat. I turned to Derrell and gave him a hug.

"Later, cuz," I said.

"Yeah, later," he replied.

I walked slowly around the back of the vehicle and paused by the door. I felt a quiet sadness as I looked over at our house. I noticed an orange-red evening sun sinking behind the distant trees. It would be dark very soon.

"Get in, Akeenah," Mum said, leaning across the back seat. She pushed open the door for me so I could get in. I slipped in next to Mum and shut the door. Her handbag rested on the seat between us.

Auntie Adele, Uncle Raymond and Derrell were standing together watching us.

"Everybody in?" the driver asked. "Let's go."

I heard him turn the key in the ignition. There was a grinding sound, which made me shiver. He turned the key again and the same screeching sound grated my ears.

"Not starting?" Mum leaned forward towards the driver.

He tried to start the car a third time.

"I can't believe this!" Mum's eyes widened.

Worry made my skin prickle. Mum got out of the car, muttering under her breath.

The driver opened his door and through the windscreen I saw them meet at the front of the car. Mum looked furious.

Uncle Raymond walked towards them. While the three of them were looking under the bonnet, I got out of the car and stood with Derrell and Auntie Adele. I began to feel nervous as I realised that it was getting dark.

I thought I heard a faint clanking noise. At first, I assumed it was just my overactive imagination.

"What's that noise?" asked the taxi driver.

"The Steel Donkey!" Auntie Adele screamed.

We looked towards the road and in the distance I could see two small red dots. Dull thuds and the eerie clanking grew louder and louder.

"Quick, hide!" Uncle Raymond whispered. "If it doesn't see Adele and Akeenah, it will go away."

We all silently crouched down behind the side of the taxi.

Derrell nudged me. "Look," he whispered. He turned out his pockets and showed me two boxes of screws. "I brought them from my dad's bag to give you, just in case you ever needed them. Maybe we can use them to distract the Steel Donkey?"

I nodded at him. I quietly lay down on the ground so I could see under the taxi. Four large hooves were getting nearer and nearer. They were like a donkey's, but parts of them looked almost metallic, glowing silvery-grey in the dark.

The monster's feet turned and I felt relieved as they moved away. *It hasn't seen us*, I thought. Then I heard a bloodthirsty scream: "AHHH!"

I scrambled to my feet as I felt the Steel Donkey looming towards us in the dark, around the back of the taxi. Panic-stricken, the taxi driver hauled himself up and broke into a run. I followed behind him as fast as I could.

"Run, everyone!" Auntie Adele shouted. I could hear she was right behind me. The taxi driver kept racing towards the road and disappeared into the night.

I thought Derrell was behind me too, but when I turned around to look, it seemed he'd vanished. Where was he? I couldn't see the Steel Donkey properly because the taxi's bonnet was open, but I knew it was at the side of the car where we had all been.

"Derrell!" Auntie Adele screamed hoarsely, looking like she'd collapse. Then I heard a noise like little rocks landing on the taxi and Derrell came dashing towards us.

"I threw down the screws," he said to me breathlessly.

I heard faint counting from the direction of the taxi, "… One hundred and five, one hundred and six, one hundred and seven …"

Derrell and I looked at each other.

"I have an idea," I told him. "Have you got more screws?"

"One more box," he said.

"Cover me, cuz?" I pleaded.

I had an idea for keeping the Steel Donkey busy for a long time – *but would it work?*

Before anyone could stop us, Derrell and I ran back together towards the taxi. I opened the back door and grabbed Mum's keys from her handbag.

I leapt up the steps and tried to unlock the front door, but my hands were shaking so much that I dropped the keys. The counting stopped. I sensed something moving closer to me. As I picked up the keys again, my hands became sweatier and sweatier.

I heard the sound like little stones raining down again. Derrell was buying me time to get inside.

"Quick, cuz!" I heard him scream. "It's nearly finished counting."

I shot into the kitchen and looked on the counter. My heart sank. It wasn't there. I opened the cupboard above the sink. I still couldn't see it! I opened another door and there it was on the bottom shelf. A two-kilo bag of rice! I hastily picked it up, slammed it on the counter and opened it. My hands were slippery and trembling. The house was shaking – I guessed the Steel Donkey was bashing at the front door, trying to get inside.

I ran out of the back door and sneaked around the side of the house, carrying the rice as carefully as I could. I was almost frozen with fear. I tried to be as quiet as I could, but I was breathing so hard I was sure the Steel Donkey could hear me. Holding my breath as I peeked around the side of the house, I caught sight of the beast's shadowy outline as it tried to get into the house through the front door.

I inched my way towards the front of the taxi. It didn't see me. I crouched down and moved slowly towards Derrell who was now waiting halfway down the road with Mum, Auntie Adele and Uncle Raymond. I clutched the open bag of rice firmly against my chest. Mum was wordlessly motioning at me, both her hands frantically beckoning me: *come on, come on.*

Then I heard Derrell scream: "Run! It's coming! The Steel Donkey is behind you! Run!"

I forced myself to sprint as fast as I could. I almost tripped over, and I felt the air behind me getting hotter and hotter. When I reached them, Mum, Auntie Adele and Uncle Raymond turned to run away, but Derrell didn't move. I turned around to stand next to him as we came face to face with the Steel Donkey.

Chapter 6

I gasped in horror as two blood-red eyes looked straight into mine. They were set in a face that resembled a donkey's, yet parts of the face seemed to be made of metal. Two long ears stuck out from the top of the monstrous creature's head. Fire flickered from its nostrils as it came slowly towards us. An iron collar sat around its neck and thick, heavy chains wound all around its body. They clanked noisily as the beast pawed the ground.

"Uhh," Derrell said throatily, as the Steel Donkey lumbered towards us. I felt really faint. I had no more energy and my tired legs wouldn't budge. My mind went blank with fear.

"Now, cuz, now," Derrell urged.

The Steel Donkey reached us, raising its front legs threateningly above my head. I shrieked in horror as I managed to summon the last of my strength. I threw the bag of rice high into the air. The grains scattered all over the road. I screamed, squeezing my eyes shut tightly in dread.

For a moment, it was as if time had stopped. Nothing happened. I opened one eye. The Steel Donkey wasn't looking at me any more. Instead, its nose was hovering above the ground. I opened my other eye.

"Is it working?" Derrell whispered.

"I don't know," I replied. We both backed away slowly. And then I heard the counting, "One … two … three …"

"It's working, cuz!" Derrell said excitedly.

I felt Mum's hands on my shoulders and Auntie Adele and Uncle Raymond appeared beside us.

"Are you two okay?" Uncle Raymond asked.

"Sure," Derrell said, brushing the top of his hair with his hand. I saw a few rice grains fly out on to the ground.

"It's counting all the rice grains," Derrell said.

My throat was dry but I managed to add, "The grains are really small too and hard to see in the dark."

We watched the Steel Donkey count the rice grains.

"This will keep it distracted all night long," I said. "There are tens of thousands of grains."

Suddenly there was a loud explosion and the air filled with smoke.

The thick smoke began to clear, until only the steam from the smouldering embers clouded the air. I panicked when I realised that I couldn't see the Steel Donkey. Where was it now?

"It's gone," Derrell gasped. "It's vanished into thin air!"

"Did all the counting make it do that?" I said, although I didn't really care about the answer. The Steel Donkey had gone!

Minutes later, another taxi pulled up and a man got out and walked towards us. As he reached us, I recognised him.

"Dad!" I yelled, and ran over to him, throwing myself into his outstretched arms.

Mum joined us and said, "Curtis, you won't believe what's happened while you were gone."

Even as we filled Dad in, it sounded so incredible. Apart from the taxi driver, Mum, Auntie Adele, Uncle Raymond, Derrell and I were the only ones who had actually seen the Steel Donkey.

I didn't sleep well that Saturday night, even though Dad promised he'd guard the door in case the Steel Donkey returned. I kept waking up, listening for strange sounds, but nothing out of the ordinary happened.

The following day, the mini van came to pick us up, and Mum, Dad and I went on the excursion, as planned. I forgot all about the Steel Donkey during the day. We played games under the shade of the tall mahogany trees and had a wonderful time eating, even though there was no rice because I'd thrown it all over the road.

The following night, I was sleeping deeply when something woke me up. I sat up, terrified, my pulse racing. I clutched my pillow to my chest.

What was that noise on the roof?

A bright light flashed in my room and I heard a sickeningly loud crackle.

No! No! Could it be …?

I fearfully turned my head towards the window. The panes rattled and I heard an eerie whistling sound. I walked over to the window and slowly peeled back the curtain. The window pane was wet and raindrops pelted hard against it.

I laughed as I realised that it was a thunderstorm. The loud battering sound on the roof was the rain. It wasn't the Steel Donkey. It was just my imagination.

I went back to bed and lay listening to the storm for a while longer. The rain stopped suddenly and I could only hear the usual night sounds of chirping crickets and whistling frogs.

The Steel Donkey really had vanished forever.

Now answer the questions ...

1 What job did Akeenah's mum do?

2 'The place always creeped me out because it was the only place in Elverton that always looked deserted.' Think of another word that could be used instead of 'deserted'.

3 On page 14, why did Akeenah try to 'create as much distance as possible between the creature and me'?

4 What happened when Akeenah and her mum went to Auntie Adele's house?

5 'I was watching him so intently' (page 30). What does the word 'intently' mean?

6 What did you think would happen when the Steel Donkey came back and everyone hid behind the taxi?

7 'Then I heard a bloodthirsty scream.' (page 38). How does the use of 'bloodthirsty' add to the meaning of the sentence?

8 Have you read any other stories about mysterious creatures like the one in this book? What happened in them?